APPLES

Life Cycles

ABDO
Publishing Company

A Buddy Book
by Julie Murray

VISIT US AT
www.abdopublishing.com

Published by ABDO Publishing Company, 4940 Viking Drive, Edina, Minnesota 55435.

Printed in the United States.

Coordinating Series Editor: Sarah Tieck
Contributing Editor: Michael P. Goecke
Graphic Design: Deb Coldiron
Cover Photograph: Photos.com
Interior Photographs/Illustrations: Animals Animals/Earth Scenes, Getty Images, Media Bakery, Minden Pictures, Photos.com

Library of Congress Cataloging-in-Publication Data

Murray, Julie, 1969–
    Apples / Julie Murray.
        p. cm. — (Life Cycles)
    Includes index.
    ISBN-13: 978-1-59928-701-0
    ISBN-10: 1-59928-701-3
    1. Apples—Life Cycles—Juvenile literature. I. Title.

SB363.M88 2007
634'.11—dc22
                                                                    2006031416

Table Of Contents

What Is A Life Cycle? 4

All About Apples 6

An Apple's Life 8

Guess What? 12

Starting To Grow 14

From Blossom To Apple 16

Endings And Beginnings 19

Can You Guess? 22

Important Words 23

Web Sites 23

Index 24

What Is A Life Cycle?

Apples are living things. The world is made up of many kinds of life. People are alive. So are cardinals, ladybugs, penguins, and tulips.

Like all living things, apples are unique. They grow in a variety of shapes and sizes.

Every living thing has a life cycle. A life cycle is made up of many changes and **processes**. During a life cycle, living things are born, they grow, and they **reproduce**. And eventually, they die. Different living things start life and grow up in **unique** ways.

What do you know about the life cycle of the apple?

All About Apples

Apples are the fruit of the apple tree. There are hundreds of different kinds of apples. Granny Smith, McIntosh, Jonathan, Delicious, and Gala are some of the most common kinds. Each apple has a different taste and **texture**.

Different apples have unique skin colors, too.

Apple trees are found all over the world. China grows more apples than any other country. The United States, Canada, Turkey, and France are other leading apple producers.

Many people eat fresh apples. But, people use apples in other ways, too. Factories turn them into **vinegar**, cider, juice, and jelly. And, people can apples for use in applesauce or pie filling.

An Apple's Life

The life of an apple begins on an apple tree. Apple trees grow best in places with mild **temperatures**. But, they also need cool weather. This is because the apple tree has different growing cycles.

Some apple blossoms are pink.

These growing cycles often follow the four seasons. In winter, the tree stops growing, or is dormant.

In spring, pretty flowers bud on the tree's branches. These flowers grow into apples. Over the summer months, the apples on the tree grow bigger and bigger.

Autumn is apple-picking time! **Ripe** green, golden, and red apples dangle from tree branches. Have you ever picked an apple to eat?

Many people enjoy eating apples.

Apples start out very small. When they reach full size, they are ready to be picked.

Guess What?

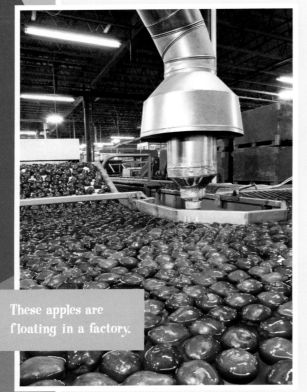

These apples are floating in a factory.

…Fresh apples can float on water. This is because they are partly made up of air.

…China grows the most apples in the world. In fact, this country produces more than one-third of the world's apples.

…Legend has it that people at weddings in ancient times threw apples. This led to the modern practice of throwing rice at the bride and groom.

…Astronaut John Glenn took applesauce on his first space flight in 1962. It was stored in squeezable tubes and was the first food eaten in space.

John Glenn ate applesauce from a toothpaste-like tube while flying through space!

…The largest apple ever picked weighed more than three pounds (1 kg)!

Starting To Grow

All apples have certain parts in common. Each apple has skin, fleshy fruit, and a core with seeds in it.

Apple trees can start from a seed inside an apple.

14

Apple seeds sprout in the ground and grow into seedlings. A seedling is a small tree. The sun and rain help the seedling grow into a mature tree.

In the summer months, apple tree branches grow tiny buds. These small buds grow a protective covering in autumn. This covering helps keep buds safe during the cold months.

From Blossom To Apple

The following spring, the tiny buds become flowers. The apple tree looks and smells pretty when it is covered with white or pink blossoms and green leaves.

Insects such as bumblebees help **pollinate** the apple blossoms. When this happens, the flowers fall off the tree. And, fruit begins to grow.

Over the warm spring and summer months, the fruit grows bigger.

In the autumn months, apples become fully developed and begin to **ripen**. When the apples are ripe, it is time to harvest the fruit.

Apples start from small buds like this one.

Many apple orchards use machines and workers to help with harvesting. Other orchards let people pick apples directly from the trees.

When the apples are picked, it is not an ending. It is a beginning! All the apples are gone. But, the tree is already growing buds and preparing for another year of producing apples.

Apple orchards grow many of the apples people eat.

Endings And Beginnings

Apple trees live for different lengths of time. Many live for more than 100 years.

When a tree is cut down, it is possible to see rings in the stump. People count these rings to tell how old that tree was.

Each ring is one year's growth.

Every year, an apple tree goes through a season of life. During that time, the same **process** happens.

Buds appear and turn into apple blossoms. Insects **pollinate** the blossoms. The blossoms turn into fruit which grows and **ripens**. That fruit is picked, and the cycle begins again.

Bees are an important part of the apple's life cycle.

Death is the end of an apple tree's life. But, it is not the end of all apples or apple trees. Because apples have seeds, they can **reproduce**. So, their lives continue on.

When a seed falls to the ground, a new tree may begin to grow. In this way, an apple helps create a new **generation** of apple trees. This is the beginning of a new life cycle.

Can You Guess?

Q: How many apples does it take to make one gallon (4 L) of apple cider?
A: About 36.

Q: What plant family do apples belong to?
A: The rose family.

The rose plant *(left)* is related to the apple tree *(right)*.

Important Words

generation a group that is living at the same time and is about the same age.

pollinate transferring pollen from the flower of one plant to another plant. This helps the plant to grow fruits and seeds.

process a way of doing something.

reproduce to produce offspring, or children.

ripe fully developed and grown. Ready to be eaten.

temperature how hot or cold something is.

texture the feel of a surface.

unique different.

vinegar a sour-tasting liquid used in cooking.

Web Sites

To learn more about apples, visit ABDO Publishing Company on the World Wide Web. Web site links about apples are featured on our Book Links page. These links are routinely monitored and updated to provide the most current information available.

www.abdopublishing.com

Index

applesauce **7, 13**

autumn **10, 15, 17**

birth **5**

blossoms **8, 9, 16, 20**

buds . . **9, 15, 16, 17, 18, 20**

Canada **7**

China **7, 12**

cider **7, 22**

color **6, 8, 9, 10**

death **5, 21**

Delicious **6**

France **7**

Gala **6**

generation **21**

Glenn, John **13**

Granny Smith **6**

growth **5, 14,
15, 16, 17, 18**

harvesting **10, 11,
13, 17, 18, 20**

jelly **7**

Jonathan **6**

juice **7**

McIntosh **6**

orchards **18**

pie **7**

pollination **16, 20**

reproduction **5, 21**

ripe **10, 17, 20**

rose **22**

seeds **14, 15, 21**

skin **6, 14**

spring **9, 16, 17**

summer **9, 15, 17**

Turkey **7**

United States **7**

vinegar **7**

winter **9, 15**